NOT NOW!

TURNING PROCRASTINATION INTO ACTION WITH A PERSONALIZED APPROACH

CATHY DOMSCH

ISBN: 979-8-89079-314-0 (paperback)
ISBN: 979-8-89079-244-0 (ebook)

TABLE OF CONTENTS

A SPECIAL NOTE TO THE READER

Are you tired of feeling stuck and frustrated, unable to progress personally and professionally?

Not Now! offers a refreshing perspective on understanding the underlying reasons for procrastination and how to conquer it. This book delves into the connection between your personality and productivity, revealing why traditional methods have failed and how customized tools can pave your path to success.

Discover a comprehensive guide that includes:

- Clear insights into the root causes of procrastination and how they relate to personality traits.

- A detailed examination of various personality types and how they influence work habits.

- Innovative, tailored strategies designed to align with your unique personality.

- Practical steps to shift from old, unproductive cycles to new, promising paths.

- Techniques to build a stress-free, procrastination-resistant routine.

Within each chapter, you will find a link to a worksheet to help you implement suggested action items. By the end of the book, you will have a complete personalized action plan to help you conquer procrastination.

Not Now! will guide you as you embark on a journey of self-discovery and empowerment. Equip yourself with transformative tools that cater to your individuality and embrace a life of growth and fulfillment. Whether you're seeking personal advancement or aiming to excel in your career, this book invites you to decode the procrastination puzzle and unlock your potential.

Now, let's get started!

CHAPTER 1

UNDERSTANDING THE PROCRASTINATION PUZZLE

Ah, procrastination—the art of doing anything but the necessary task. It's not just about laziness or lack of time-management skills; a whole psychological circus is happening behind the scenes. Let's take a closer look at how different personalities might experience this and why understanding it is crucial.

First, let's acknowledge the sneaky ways in which procrastination shows up. Maybe it is spending hours researching "the best productivity apps" instead of actually working, or perhaps it's perfecting the art of tidying up when a deadline looms. These behaviors might seem harmless—even productive—on the surface, but they delay our real goals and create a cycle of inaction.

Here is where procrastination myths come in. One common belief is that procrastinating is just about time management. If only we could schedule every minute of our lives, we'd overcome it—right? Not quite. It's more about managing emotions and understanding what makes us tick, or rather, what stops us in our tracks.

Procrastination isn't a simple villain; it's deeply personal. It can stem from fear of failure, perfectionism, or even boredom. Recognizing these root causes is the first step in dismantling its hold on us. Instead of labeling yourself as a "procrastinator," it's time to see it as a signal—a clue pointing to something deeper.

Beyond its psychological roots, procrastination takes a tangible toll. That looming sense of guilt or stress that builds as tasks pile up—it's real. It can impact your well-being, productivity, and even your relationships. But here's the kicker: understanding its nature equips you with the power to change how you respond to it.

Now that we've set the scene, it's time to move forward, armed with the knowledge that procrastination is not insurmountable.

Ready to bust some common myths and explore strategies? Keep reading because the journey to a procrastination-free life has just begun!

As we peel back the layers of procrastination, it's time to dismantle some well-entrenched myths that often hold us back from progress. First, let's tackle the idea that procrastination equates to being lazy. This misunderstanding does not recognize the complex emotional dance happening beneath the surface. Often, it's not a lack of effort but a battle against internal obstacles like fear or self-doubt.

Consider the myth that you must wait for the "right" moment to start. Does that ideal time even exist? Waiting for perfect conditions often leads to missed opportunities and growing to-do lists. While it's tempting to anticipate the motivational spark, action breeds motivation—not the other way around.

Another phantom belief is that successful people never procrastinate. The truth is that even high achievers face procrastination; they just learn to manage it differently. They recognize the triggers and develop systems to nudge themselves into action even when part of them wants to delay.

When we let go of these myths, we allow ourselves room to grow. Acknowledging that procrastination is not a flaw but an entry point to understanding ourselves opens the door to more effective strategies.

The impacts of procrastination ripple through various aspects of life. In the professional realm, it can hinder career advancement, slow projects, and limit potential. In our personal lives, we might miss out on experiences, strain relationships, or perpetuate stress and anxiety. Identifying these impacts reinforces the importance of addressing procrastination head-on.

Procrastination is not a flaw but an entry point to understanding ourselves.

Now that you have a clearer picture of procrastination's role, you are better prepared to tackle it with actionable methods tailored to your personality. This understanding sits at the heart of your journey throughout this book, guiding you to practical solutions that fit like a glove.

As we wrap up this chapter, let's reinforce our new comprehension and get ready to apply it in pursuit of progress.

Action Steps

Reflect on Your Patterns: Spend time contemplating when and why you procrastinate. Is it during certain types of tasks or when you feel a specific emotion?

Identify Emotional Triggers: Start noting any fears or anxieties that arise when you think about a task you've been putting off. Are there patterns?

Debunk Personal Myths: Consider any beliefs about procrastination that might be holding you back. Write them down and challenge their validity.

Set Small Goals: Pick a task you've been avoiding and break it down into smaller, manageable pieces. Take a single step today.

Reflect Regularly: Begin a habit of regular reflection on your procrastination habits and commit to integrating these insights into your daily routine.

By taking these steps, you are already on the path to decoding and conquering procrastination.

*To access the worksheet for this chapter,
scan the box above or enter this URL
into your internet browser.*

https://www.cathydomsch.com/chapter1worksheet

Chapter Summary

As we close this first chapter, let's recap the journey we've embarked on. We unraveled the complex web that is procrastination, shedding light on its multifaceted nature and dispelling some long-held myths.

Understanding that procrastination is more than simple laziness, we see it as a signal pointing to underlying issues like fear or perfectionism. We also explored the significant impacts procrastination can have on our personal and professional lives, emphasizing why it's crucial to address this challenge.

By recognizing the patterns and triggers specific to you, you are well-positioned to move forward with a new perspective on procrastination.

Remember, this is about understanding yourself better so you can adapt and respond in ways that propel you toward your goals.

Onward to the next chapter, where we'll dive into the root causes of procrastination, equipping you with deeper insights for your journey toward success.

CHAPTER 2

UNVEILING THE ROOT CAUSES

Procrastination isn't just a habit; it's often a tangled web of emotions and thoughts that hold us back from taking action.

One of the most pervasive roots is the fear of failure. Picture this: you're on the verge of starting a new project, but the thought of failing looms over you, creating doubt and hesitation. This apprehension can lead to paralysis, where avoiding the task seems safer than the risk of falling short.

Closely related is the pursuit of perfectionism. For some, the idea of completing a task without it being flawless is unacceptable. This mindset can trap us in a cycle of endless tweaks and delays, with the mantra "It's not ready yet" echoing in the background. However, if we pause to look at the bigger picture, isn't some progress better than none?

Next, there's the challenge of overwhelming tasks. When we perceive a task as enormous or complex, our natural response might be to put it off, hoping our future self is better equipped to handle it. Added to this mix are underlying beliefs that may whisper, "Maybe I'm not capable enough," amplifying self-doubt and inaction.

Procrastination can also serve as a sneaky escape mechanism. Sometimes, avoiding a task provides temporary relief from stress or anxiety. Yet, ironically, this avoidance often leads to heightened stress as deadlines approach—a classic catch-22.

Let's explore the concept of emotional regulation. Many of us procrastinate because we're not in the mood for the task. We wait for inspiration to strike, for the stars to align perfectly, or for some magical moment of readiness. Yet, our reliance on emotions can be misleading since feelings are fleeting, often leading to cycles of delay.

Case studies further illustrate these psychological elements in action. Consider Emma, a graphic designer who is paralyzingly afraid of not meeting client expectations. This fear led her to delay sharing her work, causing bottleneck delays for her team. Once she recognized her fear's root, Emma began implementing self-compassion practices, allowing her to see work as an evolving process rather than a static test of her worth.

Meanwhile, Alex, a diligent student, found himself trapped by perfectionism. His assignments piled up, each awaiting that "perfect" finish. He began breaking tasks into smaller, digestible parts, gradually diminishing the hold perfectionism had over him.

Understanding these roots allows us to transform procrastination into a window of insight. By reflecting on and acknowledging these motivators, we make strides toward shifting our behavior. As these real-life examples show, acknowledging what drives our hesitation opens the possibility of addressing it head-on with empathy and strategy.

Now that we've peeled back the layers of procrastination's roots, let's gear up to identify personal triggers that might be unique to you. By the end of this chapter, you'll be on your way to crafting a personal roadmap to conquer procrastination with precision and clarity.

Mindfulness can be a powerful tool in understanding and addressing the roots of procrastination.

In our exploration of procrastination, mindfulness emerges as a transformative practice, enabling us to observe our thoughts and emotions without judgment.

At its core, mindfulness involves being fully present in the moment and aware of our internal state and external surroundings. This heightened awareness can be a game-changer in identifying and managing the underlying causes of procrastination.

When we practice mindfulness, we cultivate the ability to pause and reflect on our feelings rather than react impulsively. It is this pause that allows us to dissect the triggers of procrastination. Are we avoiding a task because it feels overwhelming? Is the fear of not meeting our standards holding us back? By becoming mindful of these emotions, we gain valuable insights into our behavior patterns.

Moreover, mindfulness breeds a sense of self-compassion and reduces the grip of harsh self-criticism—a common barrier in overcoming procrastination. As we become more attuned to our internal dialogue, we can start reframing negative thoughts. For instance, when faced with a challenging task, shifting thoughts from, *I can't handle this* to, *Let me try my best and learn along the way* makes a world of difference.

A practical application of mindfulness in tackling procrastination is the practice of mindful breathing. Taking a few moments to focus on your breath can center your mind and reduce anxiety associated with looming tasks. This simple act creates a space for clarity and decision-making, helping combat the urge for indefinite delay.

Consider the experience of mindfulness practitioner Sarah, a busy professional often trapped in endless cycles of procrastination. By incorporating mindful pauses into her daily routine, Sarah learned to identify when her avoidance stemmed from self-doubt. This awareness allowed her to respond with kindness instead of criticism, enabling her to tackle tasks with a calmer and more focused mindset.

Furthermore, mindfulness encourages a shift from a fixed mindset to a growth mindset. By engaging in challenges as opportunities for growth rather than insurmountable obstacles, we invite a more proactive approach to tasks. Mindfulness, therefore, doesn't just help in understanding the "why" behind procrastination—it aids in reshaping our approach to work and life.

Incorporating mindfulness into our daily routines involves commitment, but its benefits in managing procrastination are profound. As we continue to explore the roots of procrastination, remember that mindfulness is a tool that can help carve a path toward a more engaged, focused, and productive life.

Action Steps

Mindfulness Practice: Begin incorporating a brief mindfulness practice into your daily routine. Focus on your breath for a few minutes a day to center yourself and enhance self-awareness.

Identify Triggers: Reflect on recent instances of procrastination. Use mindfulness to pinpoint emotional or situational triggers that contributed to delaying tasks.

Reframe Negative Thoughts: When you catch yourself in a cycle of procrastination, practice reframing negative thoughts by drawing on mindfulness techniques. Shift from self-criticism to a growth-focused perspective.

Journaling: Maintain a procrastination journal. Document tasks you tend to postpone, your emotions at the time, and any insights gained from your mindfulness practice.

Set Intentions: Each week, set a clear intention for one small change you want to make in response to your procrastination patterns. Track your progress and reflect on your experiences.

Using these action steps, you begin transforming procrastination into a source of insight and personal growth. As we move into the next chapter, we'll explore how identifying your personality type plays a crucial role in crafting a personalized plan to conquer procrastination effectively.

To access the worksheet for this chapter,
scan the box above or enter this URL
into your internet browser.

https://www.cathydomsch.com/chapter2worksheet

Chapter Summary

In Chapter 2, we took a deep dive into procrastination's emotional and psychological roots, recognizing it as more than just a bad habit. From the fear of failure and perfectionism to the role of overwhelming tasks and emotional regulation, we uncovered the multifaceted nature of procrastination.

We also explored how mindfulness provides the tools to understand these triggers, allowing us to reflect, respond with compassion, and foster a proactive mindset.

By unraveling these layers, we equipped ourselves with a clearer understanding of our procrastination patterns, setting the stage for tailored strategies that align with personal insights.

CHAPTER 3
IDENTIFYING YOUR PERSONALITY TYPE

As we explore personality types, it's crucial to recognize that there is no universal solution to overcoming procrastination. Each personality is unique, and understanding your type involves identifying the distinct blend of traits that shape your habits and preferences.

The Myers-Briggs Type Indicator (MBTI) is one of the most renowned frameworks, categorizing individuals into sixteen personality types based on four dichotomies: Introversion/Extraversion, Sensing/Intuition, Thinking/Feeling, and Judging/Perceiving. For example, an ISTJ, known for their structured and detail-oriented nature, may procrastinate when faced with ambiguity or a lack of a clear plan. Conversely, an ENFP who thrives on creativity and novelty might delay tasks when routine and monotony set in.

Similarly, the Enneagram provides another perspective, dividing personalities into nine types, each with its core fears and desires. A Type 1, driven by a need for improvement and accuracy, might procrastinate due to fear of imperfection, while a Type 9 could delay tasks to avoid conflict or decision-making stress.

Understanding these personality traits is key to recognizing procrastination tendencies. Are you someone who thrives on deadlines, finding motivation in the last-minute rush? Or do you need careful planning and a clear to-do list to stay focused? These insights form the foundation for developing strategies that align with your natural inclinations.

Ava, an ENFJ, prioritizes relationships and harmony. She noticed her procrastination often stemmed from avoiding decisions that might negatively impact others. She recognized this pattern and implemented boundary-setting techniques to maintain productivity without sacrificing her collaborative spirit.

For Alex, a Type 7 on the Enneagram, the love of exploration and fear of restriction led to starting multiple projects simultaneously without completing them. He structured his time to include both focused completion periods and moments for creative outlets, aligning tasks with his dynamic personality.

The DISC assessment offers another valuable perspective, focusing on behaviors and tendencies in various environments. It identifies four primary traits: Dominance (D), Influence (I), Steadiness (S), and Conscientiousness (C).

- **Dominance (D):** Driven and results-oriented, these individuals thrive in dynamic environments but may procrastinate on detail-oriented tasks.

- **Influence (I):** Outgoing and enthusiastic, they excel in social settings but might delay tasks involving isolation or detailed work.

- **Steadiness (S):** Valuing harmony and consistency, they excel in stable environments but can procrastinate when faced with sudden changes.

- **Conscientiousness (C):** Analytical and detail-oriented, they prefer having all the information before making decisions, which can lead to delays in uncertain situations.

Each DISC profile presents unique procrastination challenges and strengths. By understanding your position within the DISC spectrum, you can tailor your approach to tasks, recognizing when external support or different strategies might be beneficial.

For instance, Jake, with a high Dominance trait, balances his need for speed with precision by collaborating with colleagues who exhibit high Conscientiousness. Similarly, Emma, embodying the Influence trait, structures her day to include collaborative sessions to maintain motivation.

By examining these frameworks—MBTI, Enneagram, and DISC—you gain a comprehensive understanding of how various facets of your personality influence procrastination patterns. This knowledge is instrumental in constructing tailored strategies that harness your strengths and address your challenges, propelling you toward greater productivity and fulfillment.

Understanding your personality type through these lenses offers introspection and clarity to navigate tasks and environments in a manner that resonates with your natural inclinations. As you apply these insights, remember that the goal is continuous growth and adaptation rather than static categorization.

Beyond these frameworks, understanding your personality involves acknowledging preferences like your ideal work environment, the time of day you're most productive, and your ways of processing information. Such awareness helps you craft routines that enhance focus and joy in work.

Action Steps

Take a Personality Assessment: Use a MBTI, Enneagram, or DISC assessment to identify your personality type. Reflect on how this resonates with your work habits and procrastination tendencies.

Analyze Strengths and Challenges: Use your assessment results to list specific strengths and potential challenges your personality type may face.

Tailor Strategies: Based on your insights, develop one or two productivity strategies that play to your strengths. For example, if you're high in Dominance on DISC, set deadlines and objectives that capitalize on your results-driven nature.

Seek Feedback: Share your findings with a trusted friend or colleague to gain additional perspectives on your behaviors and receive supportive feedback.

Reflect Regularly: Continue to integrate personality insights into your daily routine, regularly reflecting on how these strategies impact your productivity and sense of fulfillment.

With these steps, you open a pathway toward harnessing your personality's innate power to conquer procrastination. As we transition into the next chapter, prepare to explore concrete tools and tactics customized to each personality type, enhancing your quest for productivity and growth.

To access the worksheet for this chapter,
scan the box above or enter this URL
into your internet browser.

https://www.cathydomsch.com/chapter3worksheet

Chapter Summary

In Chapter 3, we embarked on a journey of self-discovery, unearthing the invaluable insights that personality assessments provide in understanding procrastination. We recognized how our unique blend of traits influences our behavior and productivity by exploring frameworks such as the Myers-Briggs Type Indicator (MBTI), Enneagram, and DISC. This chapter provided a roadmap to leverage these personality insights, turning our natural inclinations into strengths against procrastination.

Understanding that every personality type—from the detail-oriented Conscientiousness of DISC to the adventurous Type 7 of Enneagram—has unique procrastination challenges, we've armed ourselves with tools for personal growth. Through real-life examples and self-reflection, we've laid the groundwork for crafting personalized approaches that align with who we are.

CHAPTER 4
CUSTOMIZED TOOLS FOR SUCCESS

Now that you know your personality type, it's time to explore strategies and tools aligned with your unique strengths and challenges. No two personalities are identical, and neither should the approaches to conquering procrastination be. Let's delve into some personalized strategies for each framework we've covered: MBTI, Enneagram, and DISC.

MBTI Types and Procrastination

ISTJ and ISFJ:

Challenge: These types may procrastinate when tasks lack structure or clear instructions.

Strategy: Structure and routine are your allies. Implement detailed to-do lists and schedules that provide the clarity and order you thrive on. Break tasks into smaller steps and use checklists for that satisfying sense of completion.

ESTJ and ESFJ:

Challenge: These types may procrastinate when tasks don't involve social interaction or immediate results.

Strategy: Engage in collaborative projects and set deadlines to create a sense of urgency. Use accountability partners to maintain focus and motivation.

ENTJ and ENFJ:

Challenge: These types may procrastinate on tasks that don't align with their leadership goals or vision.

Strategy: Prioritize tasks that contribute to your long-term objectives. Use project management tools to delegate and track progress, ensuring alignment with your goals.

INFP and ISFP:

Challenge: These types may procrastinate due to a lack of interest or emotional connection to the task.

Strategy: Infuse tasks with personal meaning and creativity. Use journaling to explore your values and align tasks with your passions.

ENFP and ENTP:

Challenge: These types may procrastinate due to a tendency to start multiple projects without finishing them.

Strategy: Harness your creative energy and enthusiasm by incorporating variety into your tasks. Use mind mapping to brainstorm and explore ideas freely. Set flexible goals that allow for spontaneity without sacrificing progress.

INTJ and INFJ:

Challenge: These types may procrastinate when tasks seem mundane or lack a clear purpose.

Strategy: Capitalize on your vision-oriented nature by setting long-term goals and then working backward to outline actionable steps. Tools like visualization and future planning apps can help solidify your path and maintain your motivation.

ESTP and ESFP:

Challenge: These types may procrastinate when tasks are too routine or lack excitement.

Strategy: Introduce elements of fun and spontaneity into your tasks. Use gamification techniques to make tasks more engaging and rewarding.

ISTP and INTP:

Challenge: These types may procrastinate due to overanalyzing or seeking perfection.

Strategy: Set clear deadlines to limit analysis paralysis. Use prototyping and iterative approaches to test ideas quickly and refine them over time.

By understanding the unique procrastination challenges associated with each MBTI type, individuals can adopt tailored strategies to enhance productivity and personal growth.

Enneagram Types and Procrastination

Type 1 (The Perfectionist):

Challenge: Perfectionists often delay tasks in pursuit of flawlessness, leading to procrastination.

Strategy: Practice progress over perfection. Utilize tools like the "good enough" checklist, where tasks are marked as complete before they're flawless, preventing delay in pursuit of perfection.

Type 2 (The Helper):

Challenge: Helpers may procrastinate on their own tasks while prioritizing others' needs.

Strategy: Set boundaries and allocate specific times for personal tasks. Use a priority matrix to ensure your needs are also addressed.

Type 3 (The Achiever):

Challenge: Achievers may procrastinate on tasks that don't offer immediate recognition or success.

Strategy: Break tasks into smaller, measurable goals that provide a sense of accomplishment. Use a progress tracker to visualize achievements.

Type 4 (The Individualist):

Challenge: Individualists may procrastinate due to emotional fluctuations and a desire for authenticity.

Strategy: Establish a routine that incorporates creative expression. Use mood journals to identify patterns and plan tasks during high-energy periods.

Type 5 (The Investigator):

Challenge: Investigators may procrastinate by over-researching and under-executing.

Strategy: Set clear deadlines for research phases and transition to action. Use a research-action balance sheet to allocate time effectively.

Type 6 (The Loyalist):

Challenge: Loyalists may procrastinate due to anxiety and overthinking potential outcomes.

Strategy: Develop a risk assessment plan to address fears and outline contingency plans. Use a decision tree to simplify choices.

Type 7 (The Enthusiast):

Challenge: Enthusiasts may procrastinate by jumping from one exciting idea to another.

Strategy: Balance your love of exploration by scheduling dedicated focus times with minimal distractions. Use time-blocking techniques to reserve periods for creative ventures and periods for execution and routine tasks.

Type 8 (The Challenger):

Challenge: Challengers may procrastinate on tasks that don't align with their vision or control.

Strategy: Delegate tasks that don't require your direct involvement. Use a delegation matrix to identify tasks that can be assigned to others.

Type 9 (The Peacemaker):

Challenge: Peacemakers may procrastinate due to indecision and a desire to avoid conflict.

Strategy: Prioritize decision-making. Tools like pros and cons lists and decision matrices can help you make choices more efficiently, reducing procrastination caused by indecision.

By understanding the unique procrastination challenges associated with each Enneagram type, individuals can adopt tailored strategies to enhance productivity and personal growth.

For DISC Profiles

Dominance (D): Embrace action-oriented tools like action boards or project management software that allow for goal setting and tracking progress. Challenge yourself with timed sprints to keep momentum high and distractions at bay.

Influence (I): Incorporate social elements into your work life. Engage in accountability partnerships or collaborative work sessions to sustain motivation through interaction.

Steadiness (S): Emphasize stability and balance by using planning tools that offer a holistic overview, like balanced life wheels. Ensure your schedule includes breaks and reflection periods to maintain a steady pace without overwhelm.

Conscientiousness (C): Leverage organizational and reference tools such as databases or detailed project plans that cater to your love for accuracy and data. Set clear metrics for success to ensure you have precise targets to work toward.

While these tools and strategies cater to specific personality types, personal adaptation is key. Experiment with different methods to find what works best for you, and don't hesitate to blend approaches from various frameworks.

Jake, a Dominance type, found success by integrating time-bound action plans and accountability partners to fuel his drive for results. Meanwhile, Sarah, an ENFP, embraced her flexibility by setting weekly rather than daily goals, allowing space for her creativity to flourish without hindrance.

Implementing these customized tools equips you with a personalized system to combat procrastination effectively. Over time, consistently applying strategies aligned with your natural tendencies will become second nature, integrating seamlessly into your work and life.

The key to these tools is flexibility and integration; blend elements from various personalities and types as needed. Consider creating a personalized toolkit that allows you to adapt to different contexts while staying consistent in the overarching strategy.

For instance, Maria, a Conscientiousness type, enhanced her workflow using Gantt charts for project planning, ensuring all details were aligned precisely. Meanwhile, Tom, an ENTP, thrived by setting adventurous learning challenges to fuel his inquisitive nature while maintaining productivity.

Self-awareness is key to self-leadership.

Action Steps

Personal Toolkit Inventory: Evaluate the tools and strategies presented and select three that strongly resonate with your personality type. Commit to integrating these into your daily routine.

Monitor and Reflect: Keep a journal of your experiences with these new strategies over the next month. Note any changes in productivity, motivation, or sense of fulfillment.

Adjust and Adapt: Based on your reflections, fine-tune your toolkit. Don't hesitate to swap or blend methods from different personality frameworks to optimize results.

Establish Accountability: Share your personalized toolkit and goals with a friend or colleague to create accountability and encourage mutual support.

Celebrate Progress: Review your achievements at the end of each week and celebrate even small victories to reinforce positive patterns and maintain motivation.

By embracing these action steps, you can transform your approach to tasks and challenges into a dynamic, personalized system that supports ongoing growth and success. As we prepare to shift from spinning circles to clear pathways in the next chapter, carry forward the insights gained here to continue your journey to fulfillment.

To access the worksheet for this chapter,
scan the box above or enter this URL
into your internet browser.

https://www.cathydomsch.com/chapter4worksheet

Chapter Summary

In Chapter 4, we took significant steps toward turning procrastination into a manageable and conquerable challenge by tailoring tools and strategies to your personality type. We explored diverse methods, from structured lists for ISTJs to creative mind mapping for ENFPs, highlighting how different approaches sync with distinct personality profiles across MBTI, Enneagram, and DISC frameworks.

By understanding that there is no universal solution to procrastination, we have empowered ourselves to experiment with strategies that resonate with our natural inclinations, making productivity feel less like a chore and more like a journey toward excellence. The variety of tools at your disposal addresses procrastination at its core and aligns with your strengths, fostering a sense of empowerment and progress.

CHAPTER 5

SHIFTING FROM CIRCLES TO PATHS

Procrastination often creates a metaphorical hamster wheel—endlessly spinning with little forward motion and a lot of frustration. However, what if you could step off, chart a clear path forward, and walk with purpose? This possibility is within reach by understanding and addressing the underlying resistance and decision-making hurdles that keep us stuck.

The first step in this transformation is recognizing the emotional and mental barriers that maintain the cycle. Fear of the unknown or comfort in the familiar often makes it daunting to change our patterns. Awareness of these feelings allows us to approach this shift with empathy rather than frustration.

- Set Clear and Attainable Goals: Break the cycle by replacing vague tasks with specific, achievable goals. Use the SMART criteria—Specific, Measurable, Achievable, Relevant, and Time-bound—to give structure to your ambitions. Instead of "finish report," try "complete the first draft of the report by 3:00 p.m. Friday with at least five references."

- Develop a Roadmap: Just as a traveler uses a map to reach their destination, a detailed plan can guide your efforts. Create a step-by-step path that outlines each stage toward your goal. By visualizing what lies ahead, uncertainty diminishes, and motivation rises.

- Embrace Iterative Processes: Understand that progress doesn't require perfection. Adopt an iterative approach, focusing on continuous improvements rather than flawless outcomes. This mindset fosters resilience to mistakes and encourages learning.

- Utilize Decision-Making Frameworks: Decision-making can paralyze progress, particularly when the options are overwhelming. Implementing frameworks such as a decision matrix allows you to weigh choices systematically, alleviating indecision and maintaining momentum.

- Practice Accountability and Reviews: Establish regular check-ins to assess progress and adjust plans as needed. Whether through self-reflection or involving a mentor or accountability partner, these reviews reinforce commitment and highlight areas for improvement.

A freelance designer, Emily struggled with indecision and felt caught in a loop of overthinking projects. By setting specific design milestones and engaging with a support group for feedback, Emily created a structured path to deliver consistent work and felt more confident in her capabilities.

Similarly, David, a Type S on the DISC, found his steady nature led to a reluctance to take the initiative. By utilizing a detailed weekly planner and celebrating each accomplished task, David transformed lingering tasks into actionable steps on a defined path.

To effectively shift from circles to paths, embrace both the systematic structures and emotional support systems necessary for progression. Trust your personalized toolkit equipped with strategies for your unique personality type while remaining open to adaptations that enhance your journey.

As you navigate this newfound clarity, rejoice in the possibilities within sight. With determination and the right methods, shifting from endless cycles to chosen paths will ensure productivity and provide a deepened sense of satisfaction and achievement.

Action Steps

Identify One Procrastination Circle: Reflect on an area where you feel caught in a cycle of procrastination. Describe the nature of this circle and how it affects your progress.

Set a Specific Goal: Develop a SMART goal related to this area. Clearly define what you want to achieve, by when, and how you will measure your progress.

Create a Roadmap: Break down your SMART goal into actionable steps, outlining a detailed plan for how you'll move forward. Include timelines and potential checkpoints.

Implement a Decision-Making Tool: If indecision is a challenge, adopt a decision-making framework to help you evaluate and prioritize options.

Schedule Regular Check-ins: Establish a routine for weekly or bi-weekly reviews to monitor your progress, celebrate achievements, and make necessary adjustments.

Engaging in these action steps sets the stage for meaningful change, freeing yourself from the repetitive cycles of delay and embracing a path of clarity and purpose. As we progress to the next chapter, prepare to build a procrastination-free routine that supports continued success and growth.

*To access the worksheet for this chapter,
scan the box above or enter this URL
into your internet browser.*

https://www.cathydomsch.com/chapter5worksheet

Chapter Summary

In Chapter 5, we discussed shifting from the frustrating cycles of procrastination to clear, intentional pathways. You've begun realigning your efforts with your goals by acknowledging and addressing the emotional and cognitive barriers that fuel procrastination. We explored practical strategies, such as setting SMART goals, developing detailed roadmaps, adopting iterative processes, and employing decision-making frameworks, all designed to guide you out of confusion and into purposeful action.

This shift is about more than just productivity; it's about reclaiming control and satisfaction in your personal and professional life. You pave the way for continuous growth and fulfillment by approaching tasks with intention and clarity.

CHAPTER 6
BUILDING A PROCRASTINATION-FREE ROUTINE

Creating a routine that counters procrastination starts by understanding the rhythm of your day and aligning activities with your natural peaks of energy and focus. An effective routine doesn't feel restrictive; instead, it provides the freedom to engage in tasks with intention and momentum, transforming your day from reactive to proactive.

- Assess Your Energy Levels: Before crafting your routine, spend a few days monitoring your energy and focus across different times. Identify when you feel most alert and when dips occur. Designate high-energy periods for demanding tasks and low-energy times for routine or restorative activities.

- Start with a Morning Ritual: How you begin your day sets the stage for what follows. Your morning ritual should energize and focus you. This could range from exercising or meditating to planning with a cup of coffee. The key is consistency—a ritual that aligns with your personality and sets a positive tone.

- Implement Time Blocking: Allocate dedicated blocks of time for specific categories of tasks across the day. This structure promotes focus and minimizes distractions. Incorporate breaks to prevent burnout and recharge throughout the day.

- Create Routines for High-Impact Activities: Identify and prioritize tasks that significantly contribute to your goals. Separate these from lower-priority tasks and build your routine around accomplishing them. This prioritization ensures your energy and focus are directed toward impactful work.

- Balance and Flexibility: While consistency is key, flexibility allows for adaptation. Life is unpredictable, and a successful routine accommodates unexpected changes while maintaining core priorities. Regularly review and adjust your routine to ensure it remains effective and balanced.

- End-of-Day Wrap-Up: Conclude your day with an evening routine that wraps up tasks, plans for tomorrow, and includes reflection. Journaling or a gratitude practice can be valuable here, providing a sense of completion and setting the stage for a restful night.

Consider Mia, who struggled with morning procrastination. By assessing her energy patterns, she realized her peak focus was during the late morning. She revised her routine, scheduling creative work for this time and opting for exercise to jumpstart her day. This realignment turned procrastination into productivity.

Similarly, Tom employed time blocking to allocate specific hours for deep work, meetings, and personal learning. This intentional scheduling of his time reduced clutter, refined his focus, and significantly decreased the urge to procrastinate.

Developing a routine designed to minimize procrastination is a personal journey. It requires observing what works, making iterative adjustments, and recognizing that flexibility is as crucial as consistency.

By anchoring your day in a routine that resonates with your natural flow, procrastination becomes less of an obstacle and more of a distant memory.

What is your morning routine?

Action Steps

Monitor and Analyze: For the next week, track your energy and focus levels throughout the day. Use this data to identify your peak productivity periods.

Design Your Morning Ritual: Develop a morning routine that energizes and aligns with your rhythms. Test various activities until you find what consistently sets a positive tone for your day.

Implement Time Blocking: Use a calendar or app to schedule dedicated time blocks for different task categories. Ensure these align with your energy peaks and incorporate sufficient breaks.

Prioritize High-Impact Activities: Identify key tasks that significantly advance your goals. Prioritize these in your routine, ensuring they receive attention during your most focused periods.

Reflect and Adjust: Review your routine's effectiveness at the end of each week. Adjust as needed to accommodate changes and continue optimizing balance and productivity.

By implementing these steps, you construct a routine that supports daily productivity and fosters a sustainable, procrastination-resistant lifestyle.

As we approach the next chapter, we'll explore how reflection and adjustment fuel ongoing growth and adaptability in your pursuit of success.

*To access the worksheet for this chapter,
scan the box above or enter this URL
into your internet browser.*

https://www.cathydomsch.com/chapter6worksheet

Chapter Summary

Chapter 6 explored the art of constructing routines that support a proactive, procrastination-free lifestyle.

By aligning your routine with your natural energy rhythms and establishing consistent yet flexible structures, you've created a framework that transforms productivity from a challenge into an intuitive part of daily life. From the significance of morning rituals to the strategic use of time blocking, each component plays a crucial role in reducing stress, enhancing focus, and nurturing well-being.

The journey to maximizing productivity and minimizing procrastination lies not in rigidity but in employing routines that adapt to your unique needs and aspirations.

CHAPTER 7
THE POWER OF REFLECTION AND ADJUSTMENT

Reflection provides a valuable opportunity to pause, observe, and gain a deeper understanding of your experiences. It's more than a tool for evaluation; it's a catalyst for informed action and personal growth. By dedicating time for regular reflection, you set the stage for meaningful adjustments that enhance and refine your journey.

- Scheduled Reflection Sessions: Make reflection an intentional habit by setting aside regular time, whether daily or weekly, to contemplate your progress. Create a quiet space free from distractions where you can think deeply and introspectively about recent accomplishments and challenges.

- Journaling as a Reflection Tool: Journaling is an effective medium for capturing thoughts, emotions, and insights that arise during reflection. Whether it's a physical notebook or a digital app, jot down what worked, what didn't, and the emotions tied to these experiences. This documentation becomes a valuable reference, highlighting patterns and guiding future actions.

- Assessing Progress Toward Goals: During reflection, evaluate how your actions align with your goals and values. This time is not just for assessing performance but also for examining the relevance of your objectives. Are your goals reflective of current priorities and aspirations? Use these insights to adjust your path as needed.

- Embracing Flexibility and Change: Realize that adjustments are not failures but growth opportunities. Incorporate a mindset of flexibility, where changes in direction or strategy are natural parts of your evolving journey. Reassess routines, strategies, or objectives with an open mind, ready to embrace necessary shifts.

- Feedback from Others: Invite perspectives from trusted friends, mentors, or peers to enrich your reflective practice. Feedback provides external insights that you might not see on your own, offering further opportunities for learning and adjustment.

- Leveraging Technology for Reflection: Utilize digital tools like reflection apps, mood trackers, or performance analytics to gather data that informs your introspection. These tools offer structured ways to visualize your journey and measure growth over time.

Consider the example of Lucas, a marketer who integrated weekly reflection into his routine. Through thoughtful introspection, Lucas identified a recurring distraction that hindered his productivity. Lucas achieved greater clarity and focus by adjusting his environment to minimize this distraction and reassess his priorities.

Similarly, Beth found that feedback from her team revealed gaps in communication. She improved both team dynamics and project outcomes by implementing regular feedback loops and adapting her strategies based on this input.

Remember, reflection and adjustment are not endpoints but ongoing processes that sustain your momentum and ensure alignment with your evolving self. Making these practices integral to your life creates a dynamic environment for personal and professional growth, pushing past procrastination with renewed energy and direction.

> *Reflection is a catalyst for informed action and personal growth.*

Action Steps

Schedule Reflection Time: Dedicate a specific time each week for focused reflection. Use this time to consider your progress, achievements, and challenges.

Start a Reflection Journal: Begin journaling your thoughts and insights during reflection sessions. Document what you've learned and how you can apply these lessons moving forward.

Evaluate Goals and Alignment: Assess how well your current actions align with your goals and personal values. Adjust goals as needed to ensure they reflect your current priorities.

Seek Feedback: Reach out to trusted colleagues or mentors to gather feedback on your progress. Incorporate their insights into your reflection process.

Leverage Technology: Explore digital tools that facilitate reflection, such as mood trackers or performance analytics apps, to provide data-driven insights into your journey.

By embedding these steps into your routine, you empower yourself with the tools to navigate your journey with adaptability and confidence, reinforcing productivity and fulfillment. As we head into the concluding chapter, prepare to embrace the fruits of your efforts and achievements in the journey beyond procrastination.

To access the worksheet for this chapter,
scan the box above or enter this URL
into your internet browser.

https://www.cathydomsch.com/chapter7worksheet

Chapter Summary

Chapter 7 delved into the transformative power of reflection and adjustment, emphasizing their critical role in fostering ongoing growth and success.

Reflection offers a moment to pause, evaluate progress, and derive insights that fuel future actions. Integrating reflection into your routine allows you to make informed adjustments, ensuring your strategies and goals remain aligned with your evolving aspirations and circumstances.

Embracing flexibility and external feedback further enriches this cycle, transforming challenges into opportunities for continuous improvement.

CONCLUSION
EMBRACING GROWTH AND FULFILLMENT

Congratulations on reaching the end of this journey! Reflect for a moment on where you started and the strides you've made. Together, we navigated the complex landscape of procrastination, explored what makes you unique, and equipped you with personalized strategies that drive meaningful change.

Your journey is not just about conquering procrastination; it's about shaping a life filled with intention and purpose. The tools and strategies you gathered are your reliable companions as you navigate the paths ahead, guiding you through triumphs and challenges alike.

Growth isn't confined to achieving goals; it's woven into every step, stumble, and moment of self-discovery. True fulfillment lies in embracing both successes and setbacks, finding joy in small victories, and building resilience. As you reflect on your progress, celebrate how far you've come and envision the infinite possibilities that lie ahead.

Think of individuals like Lucas and Beth—not just as examples but as testaments to the power of embracing one's strengths and adapting paths toward growth. Your story is no different. You're empowered to overcome obstacles, harness your uniqueness, and chart a course that's all your own.

As you look toward the future, carry forward the courage and curiosity that brought you here. Remember, this book is just a starting point. Each day presents a new opportunity to explore, grow, and uncover the depths of your potential.

Your journey doesn't end here. This is just the beginning. Whether diving into new adventures or savoring the every day, your path is yours to shape and filled with endless opportunities. Embrace this moment, and look to the future with clarity, joy, and the unwavering belief that you can craft a life lived fully—one deliberate step at a time.

Thank you for allowing me to be part of your journey. You are ready for what's next, and you've got this!

ABOUT THE AUTHOR

Cathy is an expert in personal growth and productivity and a fellow traveler on the journey of overcoming procrastination. Driven by a desire to grow and thrive, Cathy has faced the common challenge of procrastination head-on and is continually experimenting with new tools and strategies to move forward. This personal battle inspired the creation of this book—a blend of practical insights and a source of accountability.

By sharing her experiences and the lessons learned along the way, Cathy hopes to offer readers a relatable guide to conquering procrastination. The book serves both as a resource and a testament to her ongoing commitment to personal development. It's a way to ensure Cathy stays true to her advice, fighting procrastination alongside her readers with authenticity and transparency.

Beyond writing, Cathy is fueled by a passion for life's possibilities and continuous learning, always on the lookout for ways to enrich her life and the lives of those around her. In this book, she provides an open invitation to join her on this journey—a journey that values progress over perfection and embraces each step as an opportunity for growth.

Cathy believes anyone can build a fulfilling, productive life and is thrilled to share the tools and insights that have made a difference in her journey. When she's not coaching, training, or writing, Cathy enjoys spending time outdoors, soaking up nature's energy and inspiration. From hiking trails to simply enjoying fresh air, the outdoors is her go-to for recharging and finding balance.

ACKNOWLEDGMENTS

I want to thank my husband, Kirk, for his steady support and encouragement in my work and writing this book. Your belief in me has been invaluable.

To my daughter, Kierstyn, your energy and love have kept me going. Thank you for being a constant source of inspiration.

Together, you both have made this journey possible.

Huge thanks to Linda Vap from Vap Construction! When I mentioned that my book was all about procrastination and personality types, she immediately came up with the perfect title: *Not Now!* Her suggestion was spot-on and really brought this project to life. Thanks, Linda, for your wonderful insight and endless support!

www.ingramcontent.com/pod-product-compliance
Lightning Source LLC
Chambersburg PA
CBHW050514210326
41521CB00011B/2450